DETAILERS DICTIONARY

DETAILERS LITTLE BLACK BOOK

Christopher Evans

DEDICATION

To mom, for letting me detail the Pinto to try and impress a girl; and my Granny R.I.P.

I also want to give thanks to those who have been supportive, but also to those who were not.

Without both, this book would not be here today.

Thank you all

TABLE OF CONTENTS

The car that started it all 1978 Ford Pinto.
What was the first car you ever detailed?

T he definitions below are not general definitions outside the detailing industry.

Understanding these detailing terms will help ensure you have the information you need to detail at a professional level or as a reference on future projects.

Acid=/ It is used for cleaning metal rims and <u>Must</u> be diluted with water. A corrosive material (pH less than 7)

Will cause server damage to rims and other surfaces if not diluted or dwell time is too long. (see Alkaline chart)

Acid Rain=/ rain that contains a high concentration of pollutants, chiefly Sulphur dioxide and nitrogen oxide, released into the atmosphere by the burning of fossil fuels such as coal or oil and industrial fall-out.

Acid rain will cause surface damage to clear coat if vehicle is not protected or treated within a reasonable amount of time.

Abrasive=/ Natural or synthetic particles (grit or media) found in polishes and compounds that cut the paint surface to remove imperfections.

Adhere=/ To stick to. To not easily be removed.

Adhesion=/ The force between two objects that are stuck together.

Alcatara=/ Composite material generally made of Polyester and Polyurethane.

Generally used as seat upholstery.

Another form of leather like material used in vehicles today.

Alkaline=/ A cleaner with a pH value greater than 7; also referred to as All Purpose Cleaner.

All in One (AIO)=/ Intended to not only cut, but add gloss and protection in one step.

These types of products usually perform better on Light to Medium projects. Note: Some AIO's could be only two or three of the steps you may

need to take and the strength of one process may not be as effective do to other chemicals reducing the power of any one portion of another.

Alloy=/ A mix of metal & other types of material to make rims. One of the most common rim types on vehicles today.

AMPs=/ Amperage is a measurement for the consumption or amount of electricity used.

APC=/ All Purpose Cleaner. A cleaner that can be used in many situations for cleaning multiple surfaces. A pH value greater than 7. (see chemicals chart)

Applicator Pad=/ A pad used to apply product to a vehicle.

This could be a coating, sealant, wax, or anything that is applied to a surface of a vehicle, inside or out.

Backing Plate=/ The plate that is attached to a polisher. Pads are attached to this plate with hook and loop material.

Baked/Baked Dry=/ The use of heat to accelerate the drying or curing of paint, clear coat, chemicals or film.

Base Coat=/ Also known as "Color Coat," the layers of paint on top of the primer and below the clear coat.

Beveled Edge on Pads=/ Rounded corners on the edge of foam pads.

Biodegradable=/ Describes any substance that organically decomposes. These types of products are usually safe for the environment and are excepted by EPA/OSHA.

BLOOD-BORNE PATHOGENS

OSHA has focused on and issued many citations for is blood-borne pathogens. This issue ties in with the PPE emphasis, and the number of blood-borne pathogens citations was high enough that it became a site-specific targeting issue for carwashes nationwide.

In the car care industry, OSHA's focus on blood-borne pathogens may be due to the unionization push in California. When the push began in California carwashes, the unions' organization tactics included filing complaints with OSHA. The groups regularly turned in reports about employee blood-borne pathogen exposure that resulted from cleaning cars. The number of citations here increased, and the national focus on this issue was one result.

Blotting=/ The process of laying a towel down flat on a surface and lifting it straight up when drying rather than dragging the towel over the surface, to help reduce the chance of marring or scratching the paint.

Blower=/ An electric or gas power tool that forces air through in one direction. They're used to blow air into hard to reach places like cracks, crevices, grills, spoilers, and other areas a towel can't reach.

Body Shop Safe=/ A chemical which will not interfere with the process of painting a car. Usually does not have silicon that causes fisheyes, adhesion problems, or other body shop issues.

Products that are BSS are usually water or solvent based products and will not impact Body Shop.

Brake Dust=/ Iron particles from the brake pads and/ rotors.

Adhesion on wheels, with heat & lack of regular cleaning is usually when acid is needed.

Brush(s)=/ A tool comprised of either synthetic or natural bristles to displace dry particulates or agitate liquid cleaning chemicals.

There are many types of brushes. Interior brushes for carpets, fabric nooks and crannies. As well as Exterior brushes that used for rims, tires and engine compartments. Find the brush that best fits your method and process of cleaning in the most effective way.

Buffer=/ A Rotary power tool which can also be; random orbital or a dual action machine. Used to buff, polish, wet sand.

Buffing Cycle=/ The amount of time a product can be worked until it is no longer effective. At the end of a cycle the product begins to dry.

Buffer Trails/ Pig tails=/ A result that happens from improper buffing techniques on paint or clear coat, usually from a rotary buffer or when debris is trapped on the surface or a buffing pad.

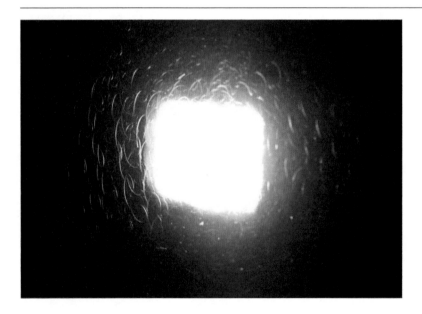

Burn=/ Is usually in reference to burning paint with high speed buffer. Do to lack of skill or focus.

Can also be Interior upholstery or chemical burn to vehicle or skin.

Carnauba=/ It is obtained from the leaves of the carnauba palm. It is formed in a paste or liquid in most automotive wax products.

Carpet=/ Synthetic fibers such as <u>polypropylene,</u> <u>nylon</u> or <u>polyester</u> are often used, The pile usually consists of twisted tufts which are typically heat-treated to maintain their structure.

CARPET CARE

A firm bristle brush is one of the most underrated tools in detailing and can be used next to loosen debris embedded in the carpets.

Start brushing in a corner and work your way towards one mid-point from all corners and sections. Once you've made a pile of debris, use a vacuum to remove it. Continue this same process for each fabric section and if you have fabric seats start with them and move on to the carpets and mats second.

After making an initial pass with the brush and vacuum, spot treat any stains with a fabric cleaner. Most cleaners should dwell on the fabric for 1 - 2 minutes, then scrub them again with a bristle brush in multiple different directions with medium pressure.

The brushes bristles will get in between the carpet fibers and help bring contaminants to the surface. At the same time the bristles will break up stains and build ups on the surface. If stubborn stains persist spray them again with your cleaner and dip your brush in a tray of hot water before scrubbing them again with medium to firm pressure. When you are satisfied with the cleaning, use the vacuum if needed to remove any visible debris.

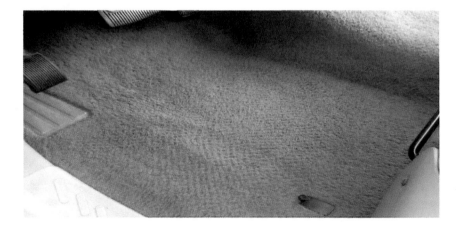

CHEMICAL BASICS

The cleaning chemicals that are used (degreasers, all-purpose cleaners, wheel cleaners, etc.) can be rated on their strength based on the pH value of the chemical. The scale ranges from 0-14, with 0 being "most acidic," 14 being "most basic or alkaline," and 7 being exactly pH neutral. Chemicals that have a pH range of 0-6 are generally considered acidic. Chemicals that have a pH range of 8-14 are generally considered basic

APC-ALL PURPOSE CLEANER

Generally, APC are basically medium to light degreasers. They're not as strong or effective as an engine bay degreaser or acid, however they are stronger than shampoo, partly because they work in a different way. Usually cleaning products "like shampoo" are formulated to remove common types of dirt in a way that affect the protective layer.

An APC is formulated to remove the common surface dirt, even if it affects the protective layers on materials. In terms of strength, you could class an APC between a shampoo and an engine bay cleaner. However, since these products are different in their chemical make-up, this is just a very loose comparison. APC and paintwork APC should be safe with any type of surface. Even though it can have an effect on the protective layer, it should not have any effect on the surface itself. So, an APC should be perfectly safe on paint, gelcoat, glass, rubber, plastic or metals. APC and fabric APC can be used safely on fabric. In fact, many APC's are very effective at cleaning seats, carpets and other types of fabric.

DEGREASERS

A degreaser is a chemical that dissolve water-insoluble substances (greases, dirt and oils) from hard surfaces. They are usually used as a degreasing agent for removing substances from engine bays, wheels, and hard surfaces. They are used to remove grease, grime, oil and other oil-based contaminants from a variety of surfaces

Degreasers can be solvent-based or containing solvent ingredients and may contain surfactants as active ingredients. The solvents used in degreasers have a dissolving action on grease and similar water-insoluble substances. An alkaline washing agent could be added to the solvent-containing degreaser to enhance its degreasing performance. Degreasers can also be produced as solvent-free, based on alkaline chemicals and/or surfactants.

WHEEL CLEANER-(ACID)

There's several factors that determine if a cleaner is suitable to use on a wheel. Hydrofluoric acid; is certainly effective and will shorten the work in most circumstances, but it's also coarse and overly corrosive, with the potential to damage your wheels and your health. Diluting acid with water will not change the pH level; It will only slow the effectiveness of the product.

Another important factor to consider when researching Wheel Cleaners is the pH level of the acid in the product. The lower down the pH scale an acid can be found, the stronger it is, and when determining wheel cleaners, stronger isn't always better.

Chrome=/ An electroplated finish of chromium typically applied over a metal or plastic substrate.

Clay Bar-Mitt=/ A soft and pliable synthetic bar that can remove contamination from smooth and non-porous surfaces (like glass, clear coat or rims). You must use a clay bar lubricant on the surface beforehand, so the bar will glide over the surface safely.

Clay Lube=/ Lubricant specifically made to ad in a clay bar to glide over the surface it is being used on.

Cleaner=/ A chemical designed to emulsify dirt or contaminants.

Cleaner Wax=/ A type of wax containing a chemical paint cleanser to remove very minor surface defects and contaminant build ups while leaving a layer of protection at the same time.

Cleaning=/ The act of removing foreign dirt/particulates/contamination from a surface.

Clear Bra / Paint Protection Film=/ Urethane film applied to painted surfaces to preserve them, specifically preventing chips and scratches.

Clear Coat=/ The clear coat provides gloss for that "wet look," plus physical protection from the elements, including ultraviolet rays. The clear coat is usually between 1.5 and 2 mils thick.

Surface Primer 0.7 mil - Initial protection layer with texture to assist the pigment layer in bonding to the metal beneath. (also see Primer)

Base Coat 0.6 mil the basecoat is usually 0.5 to 1 mil thick (1,000 mils equal one inch).

Clear Coat 1.9 mil - The clear coat provides gloss for that "wet look," plus physical protection from the elements, including ultraviolet rays. The clear coat is usually between 1.5 and 2 mils thick.

As you can see, the clear coat is very thin. So, while you can polish out scratches, you must use great care with a circular polisher to avoid burning the paint.

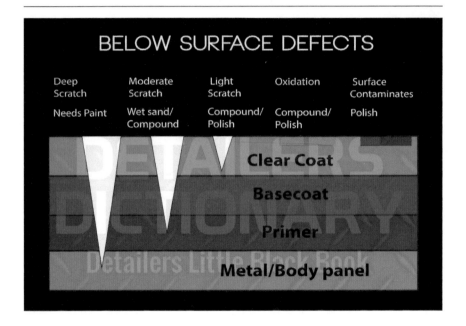

POLISHING TIPS

- First and foremost, keep the polisher moving at all times. Never let a circular polisher rest on the paint. It will burn through the clear coat.

- Work at a slow speed, between 1000-1200 RPM. A circular polisher is capable of getting very hot, especially at high speeds. While a little heat can make the clear coat more malleable, too much will burn the paint. Keep it slow.

- Work the pad flat against the paint or with the back edge of the pad tilted very slightly upward (that's the edge closest to you). This position will help you avoid dragging the edge on the paint, which creates holograms or what some detailers call "cookie-cutting".

Cloth Seats=/ Seating surfaces with a fabric/broadcloth covering.

CLOTH SEATS

Cloth seats can be cleaned using a dry-vapor steam machine or hot-water extractor. A hot-water extractor will provide better results than cleaning by hand or with a wet-dry vacuum. However, even the most powerful extractor tends to leave the seats quite damp. A dry-vapor steam machine, on the other hand, will not do this since it uses much less water than the extractor, and the steam machine only cleans the surface without soaking the foam underneath the surface.

Whether using steam or extractor, the cleaning process is similar: Spray the seats lightly with cleaning solution designed for cloth, scrub with a stiff-bristled scrub brush, and "rinse" using the machine. Tougher stains can usually be treated using the same favorite spot removers that you like to use on carpeting.

Coating/Ceramic Coating=/ Any product that adds measurable thickness to the top of paint and creates a cross linked barrier with extended durability.

Compound=/ A paste or cream containing aggressive abrasive particles designed to quickly remove noticeable defects in the paint or clear coat.

Compounding=/ Removing surface defects using compound and a buffer.

Compound Scratches=/ Scratches that are left behind by using compound. Can be removed by using a medium or light polish.

COMPOUNDS-POLISH-WAX

With the basic understanding of what these products are for lets me explain how to determine when to use what product for the job.

View these products as if you're washing your hair. Wet-Shampoo-Condition-

DRESS

- First = we pre-wet our hair; which would washing & decontamination of the vehicle(claying)

- Second = we shampoo; which would be Wet Sanding/ Compound. Heavy soiled hair needs a quality shampoo or more scrubbing to get rid of the dirt. So, compound/wet sanding would be applied if vehicles paint

- is severely distressed with scratches and heavy oxidation to flatten out the clear coat to make ready for polishing.

- Third = we condition; which would be polishing. Sometimes our hair just needs to be conditioned. So, when paint isn't in need of wet sanding or compound, we polish using medium, light or diminishing abrasives with the appropriate pad & polisher.

- Now we dress our hair. This could be gel, moss, spray or whatever your preference is will be the last step in styling your hair. Wax, sealants or coatings would be the last step in the finishing process or your vehicle. Just like your hair dressing; you use the product based on how long you want your style to last before you wash or condition it again; it's same with finishes. Wax is Only a temporary protection. The better you prepare the vehicle for its final dressing, the better result you will have, not better lasting time.

Note: Paint must be free of defects or imperfections before any final protection is applied. If not, these issues will show in the final result.

COMPOUNDS (SHAMPOO)

Compound=/ A cream, paste or liquid containing heavy, moderate, light & diminishing abrasive particles designed to remove defects such as; various levels of scratches, wet sanding & oxidation.

Compounds are the most aggressive between all reconditioning products and should be used only in the most extreme cases. They are commonly used on severely neglected vehicles and to clean up wet/dry sanding marks & oxidation. Compounds will most of the time leave behind some marring, hazing, holograms or swirls. Which is why we followed up with a finer cutting polish and pad combination.

POLISHES (CONDITIONER)

Polish=/ A cream, paste or liquid containing light, moderate to diminishing abrasive particles designed to remove light defects & imperfections such as; micro marring, swirls or light scratches.

Polishes are less aggressive than compounds in view of cutting power. There are two types: Cutting Polish & Finishing Polish. You should use a finishing polish after using a cutting polish to remove any micro-marring, hazing or holograms that may remain as well as increase the depth and gloss.

WAX

Wax=/ =/ A cream, paste or liquid containing Carnauba or Synthetic formulas designed to give temporary protection to coated surfaces. Wax Will Not correction or remove scratches, defects or imperfections.

Wax is basically like a lotion or baby oil on your skin. It moisturizes & gives temporary protection. The better you clean your body & the sooner you apply these products the better they work. Same concept with wax.

The better your finishing process is the better result you'll get with wax.

Remember that then layers & complete coverage is all you need with wax. Anything else is wasting product and makes removal more work for yourself at the end.

Wax will give a vehicle temporary protection, gloss, shine & depth to paints finish, as long as the process of decontaminating the paint is performed correctly. Wax usually last from a few car washes to 2 months. This is determined by the quality of the wax, how often the vehicle is washed, what shampoo is used to wash (ph. neutral or wax additives), if the car is a daily driver, if it's parked outside or in a garage, if the vehicle is in a hot or cold climate; also, how often vehicle is washed, and products used to wash.

The point is that just like your skin goes thru different changes that will affect the outcome of using a lotion or not, so will wax.

SEALANTS

A type of synthetic protectant, with durability that is usually longer than that of a wax, but less than that of a coating. It also enhances the appearance of paint.

This is also a protection for your vehicles paint, just like wax; although it is stronger & last longer. Let's not make the mistake of thinking sealants are a wax or a coating. Sealants usually last between 3 to 1yr. There are factors that determine the durability & longevity of a sealant like:

- Is the vehicle kept outside or in a covered area

- Various weather conditions

- How you maintain vehicle (wash)

- Type of shampoo used

- How the vehicle is prepped before application

Compound Scratches=/ Heavy and medium cut compounds leave behind their own scratches do to the abrasives in the product used to **cut** (see cut).

Concentrate=/ A product that is intended to have water added by the end user.

Contaminates=/ Air bourn particles that adhere to the clear coat of a vehicle such as industrial fall out, bird droppings, road grime, overspray.

Cross Hatch=/ The pattern created while buffing. First left to right doing 50/50 over lapping passes. Then up and down doing 50/50 over lapping passes. Once done this is one form of a 'section pass'.

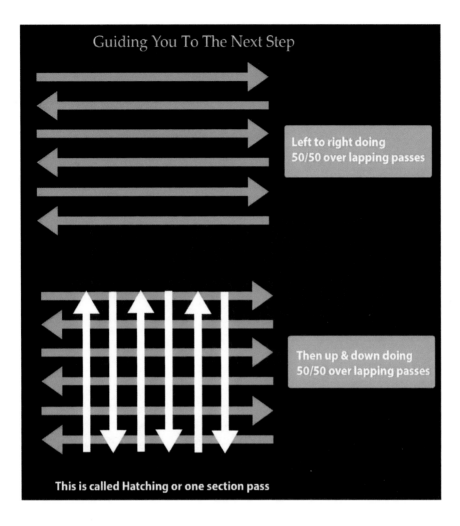

Guiding You To The Next Step

Left to right doing
50/50 over lapping passes

Then up & down doing
50/50 over lapping passes

This is called Hatching or one section pass

Cure=/ The action of a paint or coating cross-linking to form a stable matrix or film. Gases will evaporate from the surfaces during this process, so you should not protect the surface until this process is complete.

Cure time=/ The duration of the curing process, or length of time between application of a product and that product reaching a fully stable state.

Cut-Cutting=/ Removing the top layer of paint or clear coat using polish or compound. This is done most effectively with a buffer, although sand paper works as well for a more experienced detailer or practice.

Cutting Pad=/ An aggressive pad that gets attached to a buffer to help remove noticeable surface imperfections in the clear coat or paint. (see pads)

Decontaminate=/ Usually to remove contaminates from the surface of a vehicle using clay or chemicals.

One may either All Purpose Cleaner as a pre-treatment during the wash process or use clay after the wash process.

Degreaser=/ A solvent chemical designed to emulsify and flush oils and greases from a surface. Not an acid. (see Chemicals)

Detail=/ Is the performance of thorough cleaning, restoration, and finishing of a car, truck, motor cycle, RV, air plane, etc. Both inside and out, to produce a better quality and level of clean. **Detailer=/**

Detergents=/ Automotive cleaning products formulated specifically for interior and exterior cleaning of vehicles.

Dilute=/ The process of adding water to reduce the concentration of a liquid product.

Example: 3:1 ratio; meaning three (3) parts water and one (1) part chemical. Read and follow manufactures recommended subjections for their products.

Diminishing Abrasive=/ Natural or synthetic particles (grit or media) found in polishes and compounds that diminish while buffing or polishing to cut the paint clear coat to remove imperfections.

Dressing=/ A product designed to moisturize and protect rubber, plastic, or vinyl surfaces which may also contain ingredients to leave some level of gloss behind.

Note: Exterior and Interior dressing are different and should not be used on other surfaces.

Dry Sanding=/ The action of sanding without the use of water. (Also see wet sanding)

Drying=/ The act of removing moisture from a surface. The most common drying methods are Shammy's, Micro Fiber Towels and forced air.

DUAL ACTION (DA) POLISHER=/

A polisher which both oscillates and rotates. Can be used to remove paint defects or apply protection. usually more user friendly than a direct drive rotary polisher

Durability=/ Refers to longevity. Length of time a product will last before evaporating or breaking down.

Dwell-Dwell Time=/ The period time in which a product needs to make contact to start chemically reacting against dirt or stains.

DeWalt=/ A rotary buffer that has a fixed oscillating pattern. Easy to damage or burn paint finishes.

Emollient=/ A substance designed to add moisture or increase softness. Found in hand cleaners or leather and vinyl conditioners.

Emulsion=/ Stable mixture of two or more un-mixable liquids held in suspension by small percentages of substances called emulsifiers

---

Enamel Paint=/ A resin-type finish which cures to a hard finish. Can be either pigmented with color or a clear coat for a high gloss. Can be oil, water or latex based.

This type of paint is usually found on engines and brake calipers, do to being able to endure high heat temperatures.

Engine Bay=/ The compartment of a vehicle containing the engine and other mechanical components such as the alternator, air cleaner, battery, etc.

Enthusiast/DIY=/ Someone who is very interested in and involved with a particular subject or activity. Not a professional.

Environmental Protection Agency (EPA)=/ Department of the United States government responsible for protecting human health and the environment. As it relates to detailing the EPA regulates the allowable emission of pollutants into the environment from vehicles and the products that care for them.

Improper discharge is in violation of the Federal Clean Water Act that is universal across the country. Water must be collected and transported to an appropriate disposal facility or have a grease trap/catch drain that separates oil & water with a connection to the sewer. If this system is not in place with free flowing run off; you are in violation. Estimated fine after warning period is a minimum of $75,000.

Evaluate=/ To judge or calculate the quality, importance, amount, or value of something in or on a vehicle.

Extractor=/ A carpet extractor works by injecting cleaning solution and water into carpet or upholstery and then vacuuming it out with powerful suction. Some extractors use hot water.

Exterior=/ The outside of a vehicle or surface of a vehicle.

Fabric=/ A material produced from woven natural or synthetic fibers for seats in vehicles.

Fabric Protection=/ A protectant that repels dirt or liquids from fabrics.

Fifty Fifty=/ Performing any detailing work on half of one section. This is to show the result of the processes used.

Film=/ Wax build up or contaminates on the surface of clear coat.

Fine Grade=/ A term typically used to describe a clay bar or polish that is only mildly aggressive or abrasive.

In some situations, may also be referring to sand paper.

Finishing=/ The final step in the paint correction process, intended to remove any remaining fine surface defects or haze. This is where a protective coating like wax, sealant or ceramic coatings may be applied.

Finishing Pad=/ A soft pad that is used to produce a high gloss finish.

Fish Eye=/ A type of defect caused by contamination left on a surface during the painting process.

Flammable=/ A liquid chemical with a flash point below 140o degrees.

Flash Point=/ The temperature at which a chemical or solvent vaporizes and/or ignites.

Flash Off=/ Flash Off - Dwell time for solvent to evaporate from the paint surface

---

Flat Pads=/ Pads that have no grooves or dimples in the face of the pad.

Flat Paint=/ 1. Having no texture or orange peel. 2. Having little to no gloss or shine. Do not use shampoo with wax in it on Flat or matt Paint. A ph. neutral shampoo is the best way to preserve the paint or wrap on a vehicle.

Flow Chart=/

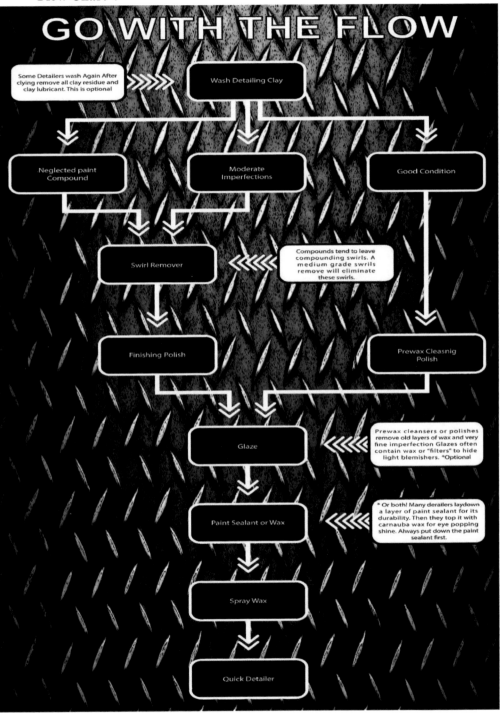

GO WITH THE FLOW

Some Detailers wash Again After clying remove all clay residue and clay lubricant. This is optional

Wash Detailing Clay

Neglected paint Compound

Moderate Imperfections

Good Condition

Swirl Remover

Compounds tend to leave compounding swirls. A medium grade swrils remove will eliminate these swirls.

Finishing Polish

Prewax Cleasnig Polish

Glaze

Prewax cleansers or polishes remove old layers of wax and very fine imperfection Glazes often contain wax or "filters" to hide light blemishers. *Optional

Paint Sealant or Wax

* Or both! Many derailers laydown a layer of paint sealant for its durability. Then they top it with carnauba wax for eye popping shine. Always put down the paint sealant first.

Spray Wax

Quick Detailer

Foam Gun=/ An apparatus that connects to a typical garden hose which uses water pressure and a soap/detergent to produce suds, usually for washing automotive exteriors.

Foam Lance=/ An apparatus that attaches to a pressure washer to produce suds from a soap or detergent to help wash the vehicle's exterior.

Foam Pad=/ A pad produced with a cellular structure (can be either open or closed cell), used in paint correction or to apply protectants or cleaners to a surface.

Foot Print=/ The actual rotating edge of the pad reaching or touching the surface area it is contact with.

Gauges=/ Pressure washer or paint thickness are the two most commonly used gauges. Measure the water pressure in pressure washer pumps or the thickness of clear coat. (see paint thickness gauges)

Gel Coat=/ A type of epoxy finish used to produce a smooth finish over composite materials such as fiberglass or carbon fiber. Usually found on boats.

Glass=/ A solid material possessing high strength and transparency.

GLASS

The first thing you should do is roll your windows down a couple of inches, so you can clean the very top of the glass effectively, also to clean the rubber. The mistakes detailer do is using too much glass cleaner. Use just enough cleaner to remove contaminants and residue on the glass. The more product you use the more you need to wipe off and causes streaking. Use a total of 2 microfiber towels to care for your glass. One towel to apply the glass cleaner and a second towel to wipe off. If you use just one towel you are almost guaranteed to see streaks afterward.

AVOID SPRAYING YOUR GLASS DIRECTLY

To prevent getting over spray on the trim pieces. It is actually best to spray the product onto the towel outside of the vehicle. Remember to use just enough glass cleaner to clean the glass, you can always mist your towel again if you need more product. Using the slightly misted towel apply some moderate pressure, slowly working the product into the glass while keeping the towel flat.

The first thing you should do is roll your windows down a couple of inches, so you can clean the very top of the glass effectively.

Another method is using a chemical free cloth. These cloths are lint & streak free. All you need is water. Rinse well prior to use, wring as much water out as possible an proceed to clean. Once done cleaning there is no additional steps, just let air dry. If an area was missed just simply fold the cloth to another side & wipe.

EXTERIOR GLASS

If your glass needs just a basic cleaning, wash it as you would the rest of your vehicle. When you are done, follow the same cleaning steps as you would for your interior glass (see above), using multiple microfiber towels and just enough glass cleaner. To give your exterior glass a deeper cleaning, you may want to consider using a clay bar. A clay bar can help remove contaminants trapped on top of the glass and in the micro-pores of the glass. The process here is virtually identical to the way you use a clay bar on the paint.

If you have very faint water marks on your glass distilled white vinegar is a good home remedy. Unfortunately, some water mark etchings are too deep for the vinegar solution to remove, so in these situations we highly recommend using a cleaner wax or glass polish. The less aggressive method first is always the safest & best practices.

NOTES:

- Use as little glass cleaner as possible to minimize streaking

- Never use ammonia-based glass cleaners on tinted windows

- Use multiple towels to clean your glass, this will help reduce streaking

- Always clean your glass when it is cool to the touch and out of direct sunlight

- Protect your exterior glass to reduce maintenance and to improve visibility during poor weather conditions

- Using a glass polish or distilled white vinegar can help remove water spots on glass

- Before cleaning the glass roll down the window and clean the very top of the glass and the window seal.

Glaze=/ A product containing a mixture of oils and solids designed to feed porous single stage finishes and/or temporarily mask minor surface defects in order to provide a high gloss finish.

Gloss=/ An objective measurement of the "shine" of a paint finish, typically representative of reflective clarity.

Grade=/ Usually in reference to grade of sand paper. (800 grit – 1200 grit)

www.gritguard.com

Grit Guard® is an injection molded screen or grid, which sits in the bottom of your buckets. It is designed to release the contaminants (dirt, grit, and debris) that you have taken off of your car and are trapped in your wash mitt or brush. These contaminants are what contribute to swirls and scratches on the surface or your vehicle.

Grit Guard® works by simply rubbing your tools across the radial designed surface. As this process takes place the particles are released and fall through the Grit Guard® and sit at the bottom of the bucket. There are no flat edges on the Grit Guard® so the dirt cannot sit on this surface.

Grit Guard® offers ... and our patented Grit Guard® Insert keeps GRIT where it belongs- in the bottom of your bucket and NOT in your mitt.

GSM=/ Grams per square meter; A measurement of weight for microfiber towels to add standardization.

Gum/ Gum Removal=/ Removing gum from interior of vehicle using steam or chemicals along with various plastic tools and towels.

Hack Job=/ Generally, this is a detailing job not performed up to the standards of a high-quality detail.

Hand Applied=/ Using an applicator or pad by hand, to correct paint or to apply product such as wax, sealants or coatings.

Hard Water=/ Hard water is formed when water percolates through deposits of limestone and chalk which are largely made up of calcium and magnesium carbonates.

Hazardous=/ A *hazard* is potential damage, harm or adverse health effects on something or someone.

Hazardous Chemicals=/ Any chemical that presents a significant threat to the environment or the health of those exposed to it without proper personal protection equipment.

Haze=/ Lacking clarity, usually describing the appearance of the clear coat. A common effect of aggressive machine polishing that can be removed with a finer pad and polish combination.

Headlights=/ Lighting which illuminates the area in front of a vehicle to provide visibility in dark ambient conditions.

Headliner=/ The fabric or vinyl covering on a vehicle's interior roof.

High End Detailing=/ A type of detailing which involves an above-average level of dedication and effort to provide the best possible results.

Holograms=/ AKA buffer trails or buffer swirls. When using a high-speed rotary buffer in the wrong way. Pad, product, lack of knowledge or training is what causes this. See Buffer Trails

---

Hook and Loop=/ Fabric that has either a hook or loop attached, when touched together they temporarily join together.

INTERNATIONAL DETAILING ASSOCIATION

The International Detailing Association is the leading industry association for professional detailing operators, suppliers and consultants to the industry. The association is dedicated to promoting the value of professional detailing services, the recognition of professional detailing as a trade, and empowering detailing industry professionals at each stage in their career.

If you are serious about your success in the detailing industry then you should join the IDA. The IDA was formed to help everyone, anywhere in the world, grow and improve themselves and their business. Whether you are an operator, distributor, manufacturer, or institution in the detailing industry, you will gain from your membership in this worldwide organization. The IDA is serious in its efforts to grow the detailing industry and wants to partner with anyone who is serious about detailing.

IDA CODE OF ETHICS

I.   A Commitment to Professionalism

II. A Commitment to the Customer

III. A Commitment to Compliance

IV. A Commitment to the Industry

V.   A Commitment to the Environment

www.the-ida.com

Industrial Fall Out=/ Also known as rail rust, embedded iron particles in the surface of the paint.

Interior=/ Commonly any part of the inside of a vehicle, including the trunk area,

---

INTERIOR TRIM

Most interior trim (dashboard, console, doors, etc.) consists of a combination of vinyl, plastic, rubber and leather, which can be cared for with many of the same products, so there is no need to get a product for each material. Some products are strictly meant for cleaning, some are just for protection and others have a combination of both.

In general products strictly meant for cleaning or protection are more effective than options that do both. If you need a serious cleaning, then we highly recommend picking up a separate cleaner and protectant. An all-purpose cleaner diluted with proper dilution ratio can be used on most surfaces or steam clean be used to address any & all trim pieces.

Insurance=/ Protection for you and a customer in case of damage, thief or accidents that may occur. As a professional this should be a required expense for your business.

Iron Remover=/ A product used to remove ferrous material that gets adhered to the exterior surface of a car.

Lacquer=/ A type of paint technology (typically single stage) which cures to form a thick, high gloss finish. Often referred to more specifically as "cellulose lacquer" in automotive finishes.

Lacquer Thinner=/ A solvent combination used to thin lacquer or acrylic paints.

Layering=/ Multiple applications of a paint or coating over a substrate, intended to produce a thicker final result or "film build." 2. Multiple applications of a sealant or wax protecting the paint or clear coat.

Leather=/ Material produced from natural or synthetic hydes that have undergone a finishing or "tanning" process. Can be finished and dyed in multiple ways and may or may not have a urethane protective top layer applied.

Leather Cleaner=/ A chemical designed to safely remove dirt and foreign oils from the surface and pores of a leather surface. Often leather-specific cleaners are pH neutral in order to avoid damaging the material or causing accelerated wear.

LEATHER SEATS=/ LEATHER CARE

Beautiful leather is synonymous with clean leather and when the leather is looking its best it is a source of tremendous pride for automobile owners. Leather seats are one of the very first things we notice when entering a vehicle and dirty seats not only look bad, but it can harm the long-term health of the seats. Modern day leather can be comprised from a variety of natural and synthetic materials. Very few vehicles actually use just raw leather and many of them have a coating on them to help protect against wear and tear. All of these materials are prone to drying out and breaking down over time so regular maintenance is essential.

Caring for virtually any type of seat involves the same basic steps which are cleaning, conditioning and protection. Inevitably over time dirt, dust, human oils, etc. work themselves deep in to the seats and can be quite challenging to remove. A good leather cleaner should be able to safely separate those contaminants and help bring them to the surface for removal. A quality leather conditioner can help keep the leather soft and flexible yet strong and durable. Cleaners and conditioners should not leave a glossy or oily finish behind. Lastly some protection can help prevent UV fading while preserving the color and finish for decades to come. With proper care the seats will look and feel outstanding year-round while increasing the resale value. In general products that clean and condition in one bottle are not as effective as a separate cleaner and conditioner. The trade off with using separate products is that it can cost more and they may take more time to apply.

A terry cloth towel using just water is the safest way the remove surface dirt. Steam cleaners can also be used to freshen up interiors if used properly.

Leather Conditioner=/ A lotion-like product designed to feed a leather Hyde with oils to keep it soft and supple and prevent cracks or rotting.

Lighting=/ Proper lighting is essential to view work performed. LED and de-fused light produce the best results.

LSP=/ Last Step Protection; the final step you take to protect the paint.

Lubricant=/ A barrier between two surfaces that add slickness to prevent marring or scratching.

Marring=/ These marks usually come from claying. Marring are very shallow marks in the surface of the clear coat that are annoying but, easy to remove.

Mat Paint=/ Paint that does not have a clear coat and lacks shine.

Medium Grade=/ Refers to the aggressiveness of a clay bar or polish, which is greater than that of a fine grade,

Metal Polish=/ A polish containing chemicals and abrasives specifically made for metal.

Metal Wax=/ A protectant for metal surfaces designed to hold up to higher temps such as exhaust tips and wheels.

Metallic=/ Small metal flakes (micas) in paint, used for an aesthetic purpose.

Metering System=/ A device used to precisely mix or dilute chemicals.

Micro-suede=/ A type of synthetic fabric made with tightly woven fine fibers, which appear similar to natural suede.

MICROFIBER=/

16 x 16 Microfiber
4 colors

Fabric produced from a blend of fine synthetic fibers (typically polyester/polyamide), designed to provide superior moisture wicking and surface cleaning.

Microfiber Detergent=/ A cleaner used for washing microfiber products that does not leave behind any detergents to help maximize the lifespan of microfiber products.

Microfiber Pad=/ A type of cutting and/or polishing pad made up of microfibers on the face.

Mobile Detailer=/ Detailer without a fixed location. Someone who will come to your location.

MSDS/ SDS=/ Material Safety Data Sheet; Information on the product you purchased. It may include information on proper use or potential hazards for the product.

Multi-Step Process=/ A series of different tasks carried out to produce a final result.

OEM=/ Original Manufacture Equipment

One Step Polish=/ A single polishing step to correct defects in the paint or clear coat.

OPMs=/ Orbits Per Minute The amount of times per minute the center of the backing plate will rotate around the center of the machine.

Orange Peel=/ A slightly bumpy painted surface that resembles the texture of an orange's exterior skin.

Orbital Buffer=/ A fixed oscillating pattern without rotation; (see chart).

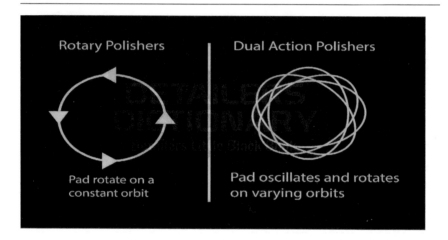

Rotary Polishers

Dual Action Polishers

Pad rotate on a constant orbit

Pad oscillates and rotates on varying orbits

Original Finish=/ A finish that was applied at the factory, not done by a body shop.

ORM-D=/ A postal service designation for products which are considered "Other

Regulated Materials for Domestic Transport Only."

This means it could be dangerous to transport due to pressure from an aerosol container or their potentially harmful/caustic nature.

OSHA

The Occupational Safety and Health Administration, an office of the US

Department of Labor responsible for the oversight of workplace safety guidelines for the use of best practices and personal protection equipment.

HAZARDOUS COMMUNICATIONS PROGRAM

Are a mandatory to have in all detail/ car washing areas. This is to educate the employee of all the various chemicals they will be using and what to do in case an accident happens. Any bottles, buckets and drums of chemicals here and there in the shop with no ID labels are a major OSHA violation and something you would be severely fined for allowing.

PPE'S

Personal Protection Equipment should be issued to each employee

- OSHA approved safety glasses

- Chemical resistant gloves

- Individual respirators or Cloth Face Mask

- Uniforms and/or aprons

- Non-Slip shoes

- Knee Pads

These are mandatory items that must be used in performing job duties in Car Washing or Detailing areas. They should be used throughout the work shift and for each vehicle car washing or detailing work is performed on.

Having safety equipment is a good thing to have and it is also a requirement. It is the enforcement and consistency of management to not only make sure employees are following policy, but also to have these preventative measures & established practices in place to limit Personnel Liability.

Overlapping passes=/ A technique utilized while applying a polish or protection where each pass overlaps the previous pass by 50% (see chart)

Overspray=/ Airborne particulates generated during the application of a sprayed paint or coating which bond to unintended surfaces.

Oxidation=/ The result of a porous material becoming dry and/or brittle due to prolonged exposure to sun and air. Often manifests itself as a dull, chalky appearance on the surface of clear coat, paint, rubber, etc.

Pads=/ There are three (3) types of pads used in the industry – Foam, Wool and micro fiber. Each pad is used in various processes and with various polishers.

Pad Washer=/ Cleaning tool to used to remove residue and other elements from micro fiber, wool and foam pads.

Paint Cleaner=/ A chemical which uses solvents and/or very mild abrasives to remove contaminants from painted surfaces, preparing them for further polishing or the application of a protective product.

Paint Defects=/ Are the issues within the paint itself. These are caused by issues during the painting process.

Not to be confused with Paint contamination.

Paint Gauges=/ Precision instruments which use either mechanical or electronic means to measure the thickness of paint film applied over a substrate. Measuring the depth of your paint will allow you see how thick the clear coat is, which will help you determine exactly how to treat it.

Paint Preparation=/ The process of readying paint for a wax, sealant, or coating. This can include washing, decontamination, compounding, and polishing.

Paint Protection=/ Most common protection are: wax, sealants, ceramic coatings and vinyl wraps.

Paint Sealer=/ See Paint Cleaner

Surface Primer 0.7 mil - Initial protection layer with texture to assist the pigment layer in bonding to the metal beneath. (also see Primer)

Base Coat 0.6 mil the basecoat is usually 0.5 to 1 mil thick (1,000 mils equal one inch).

Clear Coat 1.9 mil - The clear coat provides gloss for that "wet look," plus physical protection from the elements, including ultraviolet rays. The clear coat is usually between 1.5 and 2 mils thick.

Paint Thickness Gauge=/ Is a device used to measure the thickness of clear coat, paint, rust. This tool will aid you in determining if previous body work has been performed and to inform you of how much clear coat you have to work with before sanding or compounding in a particular area on painted surfaces.

Panels=/ Different sections on a vehicle example: fender, doors, trunk.

Pass/Passes=/ (See Section Pass)

Pet Hair/ Removal=/ To remove pet hair with Stones, Rubber Brushes, rubber gloves and vacuum cleaners are the most common ways to get rid of hair. It is very time consuming to accomplish this task.

Ph Scale=/ A numeric scale ranging from 0-14 which describes the acidity or alkalinity of a substance. A pH of 7 is considered neutral. A very important fact to remember about the pH of a chemical is that it

does not change by adding water. Example: an acid wheel cleaner may have a pH of close to 0. Diluting the acid with water according to the label directions will not change that pH value. What will change is the speed the chemical will reacts with the surface it is used on.

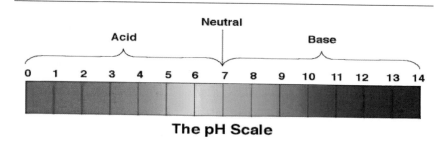

The pH Scale

Pig Tail=/ A pattern of deep scratches, resembling a pigs curly tail, most often caused by trapped particulates during the process of sanding or polishing with a Dual Action Polisher.

Plastic=/ Material made of synthetic or organic compounds with a moderate to low melting point which is easily molded into a variety of forms. Often used both inside and outside automobiles due to its relatively good durability, lightweight and low cost.

Pneumatic=/ Describes a type of power tool which is powered by a high volume of compressed air.

Polish=/ A liquid or paste with suspended abrasive particles intended to remove mild to moderate defects from a surface and refining its finish.

Polisher=/ A power tool that is usually a Random Orbital or Dual action polisher used to correct medium to light defects on paint and to apply protection.

Polishing Pad=/ A medium grade pad designed to work with a polish to remove moderate surface defects.

Polymer=/ A chemical compound found in synthetic waxes and other chemicals.

Pressure/Pad Pressure=/ The amount of pressure one places on a polishing machine. Which is usually 5-7 lbs. of pressure.

Pressure Washer=/ A high pressure water machine that sprays. It is used to wash dirt and other contaminates off vehicles.

Primer=/ Material applied to the surface to seal, fill scratches and improve adhesion of paint.

Pre-Wash-Prep Wash=/ The use of chemicals such as tar removers, degreasers, iron dissolvers, or soap to help clean prior to starting the normal wash process.

Professional=/ A person fully educated, trained and skilled in all aspects of his profession.

Professional Detailer=/ A person who is capable of cleaning, polishing and protecting an automobile at a high level while acting in a professional manner in all aspects of their business.

The IDA International Detailing Association is a great place to find a professional detailer.

Procedure/Processing=/ To put through the steps of a prescribed method of application techniques.

Protection=/ Any product which provides a sacrificial barrier between the environment and a vehicle's material surfaces, slowing natural deterioration.

PSI=/ Pounds per Square Inch, a measure of pressure which can apply to gases or liquids.

Quick Detailer=/ A liquid product designed to add lubricity between a towel and surface, allowing the safe removal of dust or oils on a surface. These products may also contain gloss enhancers or some protection.

Rail Dust=/ Red or rust color spots on the finish that can penetrate deep into the clear. Caused from transport or embedded brake dust.

Random Orbital Buffer=/ A power tool which attaches to a backing plate and buffing pad that uses random oscillation to spread a product onto a surface and/or utilize an abrasive to remove surface defects from a surface.

Recondition=/ To restore to good condition by repairing. Using various tools, parts and processes.

This

Refinish=/ To put on a new finish or final coat.

In detailing this usually means wet sanding or compounding a vehicles surface to apply a protection.

Resin=/ Thick liquid which is most often used to harden composite materials such as fiberglass or carbon fiber. 2. A liquid ingredient in some protective coatings and sealants.

Restoration=/ Bringing something back to its original condition.

Restore=/ To bring back to a previous or original condition.

RIDS=/ Random Isolated Deep Scratches; random in the fact that there is no "pattern" to the scratches.

Rinse less Shampoo=/ A type of shampoo that is typically low sudsing and high in polymers to provide lubricity without the need to flush away excess residue with water.

Rotary=/ A buffer that has no secondary action to its rotation.

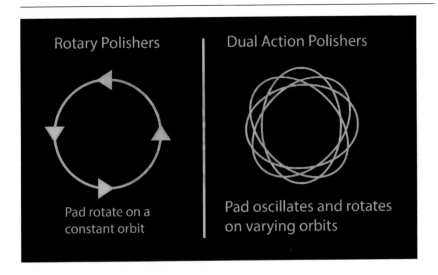

The best way to determine if a vehicle needs buffing or polishing is by: Physically look at the paint condition.

If the vehicle is oxidized, has medium to heavy scratches its needs buffing.

If the vehicle has light to medium defects or just needs a shine; a cutting polish will work fine.

Look at any vehicle before you commit to an assignment an always ask if issues on the paint should be corrected or just polished.

RPMs=/ Revolutions Per Minute; How many times in a minute the backing plate on a rotary machine rotates.

Rupes Brand=/ Rupes has many products worldwide, from their LHR15ES and LHR21ES polishers are well known to the detailing community and they show the exact type of quality and innovation that Rupes has been known for.

Sanding=/ The use of various grits of sandpaper to remove material from a surface.

Section Pass=/ (see section pass chart)

Scratches=/ Below surface defects which typically appear linear in nature.

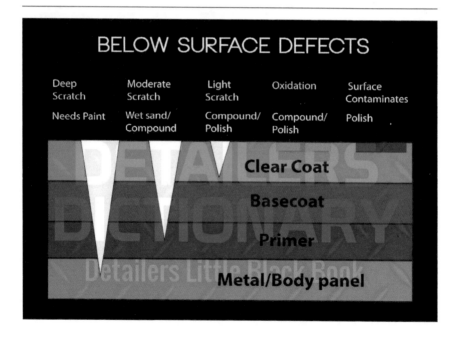

Sealant=/ A type of synthetic protectant, with durability that is usually longer than that of a wax, but less than that of a coating. It also enhances the appearance of paint.

Semi-Permanent Coating=/ A strong, cross-linked film that is typically based on strong base elements (e.g. silica, ceramic) which is more resistant to degradation than a sealant or wax.

Schuff-Schuff Marks=/ Marks that have been transferred onto a vehicle by a hard object, leaving behind damage that disfigures the over-all appearance of a vehicle

Shampoo=/ A liquid or gel which contains a surfactant and a co-surfactant designed to help loosen dirt and contaminants and create a slick surface, so the paint is not easily marred while washing.

Sheeting Method=/ A drying technique using water to dry the car. Using an open-ended hose, at a low pressure, you flow water from the higher surfaces down. This cascade effect of water can remove 80+% of water from the surface of your car.

Shine=/ A subjective term typically used to describe a surface with high gloss and reflective properties.

Short Cycle=/ To not fully work the polish. Fast arm movement, and not allowing the polish to fully do its intended job to correct or finish paint.

Single Stage Paint=/ Has color and clear added together. Most vehicles prior to 1980's have this type of paint.

Silicate=/ A hard glossy compound that usually has a form of the dioxide. This chemical is used in waxes, polishes and dressings. Paint that does not require clear coat.

Silicone=/ A group of synthetic and natural compounds that have a high resistance to heat and water. Silicone may cause serious issues in body shops. Non-silicone products are preferable for body shop usage.

Synthetic=/ A chemical synthesis made to imitate a natural product.

Soft Start=/ The function of a machine to not immediately go to the full selected speed or RPMs/OPMs.

Solution Finish=/ A plastic and trim restore to bring back the life of faded plastic surfaces.

Solvent=/ A chemical substance which dissolves other dissimilar chemicals.

Spindle Threads=/ The threaded connection between a polisher's spindle/arbor and a backing plate, measured in size and pitch.

Spray on Protection=/ Any sealant, wax, or coating which can be atomized for easy application.

Spray on Sealant=/ A form of spray on protection with properties similar to a traditional polymer sealant.

Spur=/ Tool used to clean the residue build up on buffing pads.

Steam Cleaner / Steamer=/ A tool that uses a boiler to generate pressurized, high temperature water vapor which can be used to clean or emulsify soluble substances with minimal saturation. Also, useful to destroy mold spores and bacteria.

Streaks=/ Remaining residue left behind after you have attempted to wipe away excess product.

Strip/Stripping=/ Removing all oils, polishes, waxes or fillers from the paints surface.

Surface=/ The top and outer most layer of any material.

Surfactant=/ A compound often used in shampoos, soaps, all-purpose cleaners, and degreasers to emulsify and carry dirt and contaminants away from a surface.

Swirls/ Swirl Marks=/ Random, circular below-surface defects, which cumulatively often resemble a spider web when viewed under direct lighting.

Synthetic Leather / Leatherette=/ Artificial leather. A man-made product to resemble real leather.

Synthetic Wax=/ Has chemical polymers that are made to imitate natural wax.

Tape=/ Usually low tack masking style tape used to protect trim from being hit with a pad during correction or polishing.

Technique=/ The way to carrying out a particular task, especially in the execution and performance of a specific procedure or process.

Technician=/ A person skilled and knowledgeable in the work he/she is to perform in detailing a vehicle. A person skilled in the art of the craft.

Test Spot=/ A test spot that is not obviously seen to make sure product will not bleed or damage surface you're working on.

Three Step=/ A paint correction process comprised of three distinct stages of defect removal; can describe any combination of sanding, compounding, or polishing procedures to produce a refined finish.

Throw=/ The distance the center of the backing plate travels in reference to the center point of the head of the machine.

Tint=/ Film applied to the interior of vehicles for protection to block out the sun and UV rays.

Tint Removal=/ Removing tint film from a vehicle using various methods such as: steam, adhesive removers with plastic or steel blades.

Top Coat=/ The top layer of paint that is the color coat on modern paint finishes and the clear coat on basecoat/clearcoat paint finishes.

Tornado Brand=/ Featuring patented tornado like air movement Tornado has come up with some real detailing game changers. From cleaning guns that take any cleaning solution and make them a foam, to a foam gun to use on the exterior of your car, to a simple blower,

---

Trim=/ Metal, vinyl, leather or plastic components on a vehicle's interior or exterior which are attached to the main body, intended for protection or ornamentation.

Two Bucket Method=/ An approach to traditionally washing a car which employs separate buckets for soaping and rinsing a wash mitt, sponge, or brush.

Two Stage Paint=/ This is were a base coat of color is applied and then a second coat of clear is sprayed and orange peel is sanded and buffed.

Two Step=/ A paint correction process comprised of two distinct stages of defect removal; typically, one step of compounding and one step of polishing, but can describe any combination of either.

UV 'Ultraviolet' Light=/ Light that can cause many biological substances to glow.

UV Rays=/ Also referred to as Ultraviolet Radiation, UV has a shorter wavelength than visible light. UV exposure can cause the degradation

of many automotive materials such as paint, rubber, vinyl, and leather unless adequate protection is present.

Vacuum=/ A tool which employs an electric motor to generate suction, used to collect either wet or dry dirt and grime.

Vehicle Safety=/ Appropriate policy that will identify personnel that will have access & permission to move vehicles. Having very clear policies about moving vehicles should include:

- Have a second person keep watch as the vehicle is moved if applicable

- Walk completely around the vehicle before moving it to check for items that might be run over

- Tap the horn and check all mirrors before moving the vehicle

- Do not move the vehicle with the driver door open or with any equipment on the car.

- Make sure parking brake is applied

- Vehicle keys should never be left inside

- Vehicles should always be lined up in designated work stations

Vinyl=/ A form of plastic polymer often used to produce dashboard, door panel, and seat coverings as well as convertible tops.

Waffle Weave=/ A type of towel or pad with a surface containing "pockets" or waves, similar in appearance to a breakfast waffle.

A type of microfiber towel typically used for drying a vehicle after washing, or for streak-free glass cleaning.

Wash Media=/ The tool used to wash the exterior of your vehicle.

Wash Mitt=/ A type of wash media consisting of natural or synthetic fibers as opposed to a foam sponge material. There's typically a place to put you hand inside, hence the term "mitt".

Washing=/ The cleaning of the vehicle's exterior in order to prep it for the following steps, usually the decontamination step.

Water Based=/ A product that has water as the main ingredient as opposed to an oil or silicone.

Water Marks=/ The minerals that are left over when hard water evaporates. These can lead to the physical etching which can cause serious damage to a vehicle's exterior surfaces.

Water Purification=/ Removing minerals and elements from hard water through a filtering system.

Water Soluble=/ Something that is able to dissolve in water.

Water Spot Remover=/ Product that is used to remove minerals on the surface after water has dried.

Waterless Wash=/ A product with a high concentration of polymers designed to quickly emulsify and encapsulate dirt and grime for safe removal with minimal water usage.

Watts=/ or Wattage is a measure of the amount of work electricity does. Volts x Amps = Watts.

Wax-Waxing=/ A natural substance harvested from various organic palm sources which can be applied to paint and other glossy surfaces to provide protection.

Light surface protection that gives gloss and shine if properly treated before applying. Wash, clay and polish if needed to produce better results.

Weathering=/ Descriptive term for the effects of deterioration due to environmental exposure.

Having a vehicle exposed to the elements over time, with no protection will adversely affect the condition.

Wet Sanding=/ The act of sanding clearcoat with wet sand paper of various grits, to remove surface defects.

This task is usually performed by skilled professionals.

WASHING

Everything begins with washing; whether it's Detailing or simple maintenance. This is one of the most overlooked and most important aspects of detailing. Imperfections that occur in paint surfaces such as swirls, scratches & water spots happen during the washing and drying process.

Using various methods to properly wash a vehicle, along with the right products, tools & techniques you can eliminate or reduce these issues. In this section you will learn about:

- Pre-Wash Decontamination

- Iron Removers

- Clay Bar/ Mitt

- Two Bucket Wash Method

PRE-WASH DECONTAMINATION

When there is heavy built on a vehicle you will want to use a stronger cleaner than just your wash shampoo; like an all-purpose cleaner. This will help break up and loosen dirt, tar, sap, bird droppings, and other stubborn forms of contamination. It is recommended to degrease before you shampoo a vehicle. As you shampoo your vehicle, this will ensure there is no cleaner remaining on your vehicle after the final rinse. It's important that you know most cleaners will usually remove layers of protective sealant or wax; so, an all-purpose cleaner isn't needed every time. You'll also need to re-apply your coat(s) of protection afterwards.

IRON REMOVERS

Iron removers will effectively and safely dissolve iron buildup on or in the paint. Using an iron remover reduces the need for a clay bar or clay mitt.

Iron removers are not a substitute for using clay; it is to aid in the removal of deeply embedded contaminates that clay bar alone will not remove. Only use this product **out of direct sunlight.**

CLAY BAR/ MITT

Clay Bar or Clay Mitt is a pliable synthetic substance in the form of a bar or layered onto a wash mitt that is used to remove contaminates from non-porous surfaces like paint, glass & rims.

"Clay Bar/Mitt **will not remove scratches or swirls**". Clay is used after a vehicle has been washed and you should only use light pressure when claying. The more pressure you use the more chances of marring the paint.

Each of these decontamination methods will vary depending on the condition of the paint and can be used individually or in a combination. The purpose of any of these processes is to ensure the paint is as free of any type of contaminates as possible. The cleaner the paint will make any buffing, polishing or protection easier to apply.

WASHING & DRYING

Two Bucket Method

The two-bucket method of washing a vehicle is the safest way to wash by minimizing the possibility of adding imperfections onto paint surfaces.

- One bucket is used for shampoo

- Second bucket is used to rinse

- A third bucket should be used separately for rims & tires. Never cross contaminate any of these buckets.

Grit Guards **are a must** when using any bucket. They trap debris, dirt and contaminates at the bottom of the bucket, so they are not redeposited back into your wash medium. This is one of the main sources of swirls & scratches in paint. It should also be noted that when washing only little to no pressure should be used while washing.

Start from the top & work your way down, flip the wash mitt after every panel. Rinse mitt after every two panels and make sure to run the mitt across the grit guard.

DRYING

Drying is the other biggest source of swirls & scratches on paint surfaces. It is best to blow air in those nooks & crannies before and or after drying to help prevent that continuous drip run.

Microfiber & shimmies are recommended because they don't leave behind lint like a cotton towel will & they both hold 4 to 5 times its weight in water. Avoid dragging the towel as much as possible (blot Dry) and use only light pressure.

Before any drying method is used CHECK to ensure towel is clean & free of contaminates; and the blower is also free of embedded debris and has a rubber tip.

Water Based=/ A product that has water as the main ingredient as opposed to an oil or silicone.

Water Marks=/ The minerals that are left over when hard water evaporates. These can lead to the physical etching which can cause serious damage to a vehicle's exterior surfaces.

Water Purification=/ Removing minerals and elements from hard water through a filtering system.

Water Soluble=/ Something that is able to dissolve in water.

Water Spot Remover=/ Product that is used to remove minerals on the surface after water has dried.

Waterless Wash=/ A product with a high concentration of polymers designed to quickly emulsify and encapsulate dirt and grime for safe removal with minimal water usage.

Watts=/ or Wattage is a measure of the amount of work electricity does. Volts x Amps = Watts.

Wax-Waxing=/ A natural substance harvested from various organic palm sources which can be applied to paint and other glossy surfaces to provide protection.

Light surface protection that gives gloss and shine if properly treated before applying. Wash, clay and polish if needed to produce better results.

Weathering=/ Descriptive term for the effects of deterioration due to environmental exposure.

Having a vehicle exposed to the elements over time, with no protection will adversely affect the condition.

Wet Sanding=/ The act of sanding clearcoat with wet sand paper of various grits, to remove surface defects.

This task is usually performed by skilled professionals.

WHEELS AND TIRES=/

When cleaning your wheels and tires it is important to you have the proper tools and products. It is also important to know what type of wheels you have so you use the proper products on them. If they are factory alloy wheels, chances are they have a layer of clear coat on them.

This makes things easy because you can use a variety of wheel cleaners without worrying about oxidizing the wheels finish. You may also treat them as if it's like your clear coat on your paint, meaning you can wash, polish and protect your wheels. After market or upgraded wheels that have a high polished finish or bare metal need to be treated carefully, otherwise you may etch or stain the finish and cause perminate damage the wheels.

The wheels should be completely cool when you start to clean them. If the vehicle has been driven, even just a test drive, give them time to cool down before using any cleaner on them. A cold-water rinse will help cool them down quicker. Clean the wheels in the shade whenever possible to avoid water marks or rinse them frequently while in direct sunlight.

The best way to clean and maintain your wheels and tires is by using auto-motive shampoo and water with a dedicated wash mitt. This is safe for every type of wheel finish and reduces the use of wheel cleaners (unless needed).

Soap and water will help remove loose contaminants and clean wheels that are well maintained but brake build up will require a wheel cleaner. The safest bet is to use your Degreaser as a pre-treat. It can be used on any type of wheel finish and you can increase the cleaning power by letting the product dwell for several minutes if you are in the shade. Acidic wheel cleaners are highly effective, but they can easily oxidize or stain polished wheel finishes. Acidic wheel cleaners should only be used on factory wheels with a thick clear coat on them.

When you are done rinse the wheels with a steady stream of water to remove any remaining residue. Using a brush with stiff bristles can cause damage to finished rims, brushes with soft bristles or natural fibers would be safer. If you still have some remaining stains, try a metal polish or finishing polish which can be applied to most bare metals and clear coated rims.

TIRES

Use a dedicated wash mitt or sponge and stiff bristle brush for tires. Wash them with soap and water and degreasers if they need a deeper cleaning. To get the best results for your dressing, it is recommended cleaning the tires with a degreaser and a firm brush.

Soak your tires with the degreaser and allow it to penetrate for a couple of minutes. Scrub your tires with the brush to remove the heavy contamination. Then apply tire dressing.

Simply apply tire dressing onto an applicator pad and work it into your tires; never spray tire directly as you may get over spray on rims, paint or floor. Use as little product as possible to prevent sling onto your paint. You are better off applying multiple thin coats of tire dressing than one thick coat. For complete even coverage, move your vehicle forward or backwards to apply dressing on the part of the tire that was closest to the ground.

Note: In places where body shop work is performed a water- based dressing should be use.

Wool=/ Natural or synthetic material typically used to produce a polishing pad for aggressive defect removal.

Detailer Helper=/ Detailing belt to store tools and products that will save you time and money.

FACTS & TIPS

WASHING

- Use as little pressure as possible with your wash medium

- Allow the shampoo to do most of the cleaning, not your force

- Using a foam gun to pre-soak your vehicle can help minimize adding imperfections

- It's always best practice to wash and dry in the shade, out of direct sunlight

- Always use two wash buckets, one with shampoo and water, and one with rinse water

- Using a Grit Guard insert helps release contamination from your wash mitt

- Use a separate wash media for your wheels and tires, heavy contaminated areas, and lightly contaminated areas

- Pre-treat heavily contaminated areas of your vehicle with water or APC

- Rinse your wash media as frequently as possible (every panel or so)

- The more contaminated your vehicle is, the more often you should rinse your mitt or sponge

- It's good practice to wash weekly or every two weeks

- Using a shut off valve allows you to quickly remove a hose nozzle without getting wet or running to the water source

- You can use a second Grit Guard insert in each bucket with shampoo and water

- Some shampoos can be used to strip off previous coats of protection when used in high concentration

- Using a Grit Guard insert helps trap contamination on the bottom of the bucket

- Utilize the sheeting method to remove most of the water from your vehicle

- A micro fiber drying towel is the safest product to use to dry your vehicle

- Instead of wiping with your drying towel, blot the paint to minimize adding imperfections

- Using a blower can help remove water between panels, mirrors, gaps, lug nuts and other hard to reach areas

CLAY BAR

- If you drop a piece of clay, throw it away!

- Working on a small area ensures that your clay lube will not dry up too fast

- Do not use too much pressure when gliding a clay bar across the lubricated surface

- Using a quick detailer that leaves behind a slick surface is often good as a clay bar lubricant

- For most vehicles, we recommend using a fine grade clay bar

- A medium grade clay bar will almost always leave behind some marring that needs to be polished to remove

- Optimum No Rinse mixed with water is a common clay bar lubricant amongst professionals

- You can often tell if there is contamination still on the surface by listening closely as your clay

- Avoid using a clay bar in direct sunlight so that your clay lube does not dry up quickly

- Cutting your clay bar into small pieces helps preserve your clay in the event you drop a piece

- Always try to reshape your clay to expose a fresh, clean piece of clay

- When storing your clay bar, mist some of your clay lube in the bag or container to keep is soft and flexible

- It's good practice to re-wash your vehicle after using a clay bar to remove any loosened contamination and to remove excess clay bar residue

- Clay not only works well on your paint, but also your glass, wheels, plastics and other surfaces

POLISHING

- The smaller the section you work in, the better your results will be

- Do not rush the polishing process, it is very time consuming, but the results are worth it

- When using a random orbital or dual action buffer, apply roughly 15 - 20 lbs. of pressure

- Always match the aggressiveness of the product with the aggressiveness of the pad

- Swap out your pad for a fresh one every couple of panels for maximum results

- Keep a bucket of water and Snappy Clean solution by your side to soak your pads as soon as you are done

- Using the proper lighting when polishing is important to assess your results accurately

- Smaller pads offer you more control and can get in tighter areas

- Larger pads can spread products quickly, which is great when applying a sealant

- Rotary buffers should be used by experienced detailers and professionals

- Tape off your trim, glass, and any other area you do not want polish to potentially damage

- Use 3 pea sized drops of polish per working area, many detailers use too much product

GLAZES

Glazes can help increase the depth and gloss in the paint

- The filling of light imperfections is only temporary and will return over time

- Do not expect a glaze to fill in too many imperfections, only the slightest imperfection can be masked

- Glazes typically cannot be layered, so only one coat is necessary for maximum results

SEALANTS

- In general, sealants last somewhere between 3 to 6 months

- When applying a sealant, it's best to spread it as thin as possible

- In general, you should give each coat of sealant at least 1 hour to cure and bond to the paint

- Sealants can be layered to increase the depth and gloss as well as protection

- Sealants can be topped with a wax to get the best of both worlds in terms of looks and durability

COATINGS

Most coatings are intended to protect the paint, but there are also options for wheels, glass, plastic, vinyl, leather, fabric, etc. Generally speaking, the application process is very similar for all coatings and for all areas of the car. You want to heed the manufacturer's instructions because a mistake in coating application can cost you in terms of both time and money.

WAX

- Carnauba waxes typically last between 3 to 8 weeks

- Apply your wax as thin as possible, only a microscopic layer of wax actually sits on your paint, excess wax is just wasted

- In general, you should give each coat of wax 1 to 24 hours cure time

- It is best to work in the shade when applying and removing a wax

- Most waxes can benefit from 2 to 3 layers for maximum depth and gloss

- When your paint stops beading water, it is time to reapply a coat of wax

TOWELS

- Always remove any tags on microfiber products to minimize the risk of marring the paint

- Always wash new microfiber towels prior to using them for the first time

- Never use fabric softener when washing or drying your towels

- Group your towels together, such as paint safe towels, wheel and tire towels, interior towels, etc.

- Adding distilled white vinegar to your rinse cycle can help further clean your microfiber

- If your towels lose their absorbency, try boiling them to dissolve product and reopen the pores

- Store your clean microfiber towels in labeled microfiber storage bags

- Always wash your microfiber with microfiber, avoid mixing them with other fabrics

TIRES

- Silicone based tire dressings have a higher tendency to sling up onto your paint

- Water based tire dressings get absorbed into your tires and nourish your rubber

- Properly prepping your tires prior to applying a dressing can increase durability and prevent tire dressing sling

- Always apply your tire dressing in thin, even coats

- Drive your vehicle a few feet forward after applying the first coat of dressing so you can get an even application on the part of the tire that was closest to the ground

WHEELS

- Maintain your wheels with shampoo and water with a dedicated wash media

- Keeping a coating of protection on your wheels will make maintaining them significantly easier

- Always use a pH balanced wheel cleaner when dealing with after-market wheels

- Acidic based wheel cleaners can easily oxidize a high polished finish

- Using a clay bar can effectively prep your wheels for polishing and protecting

- Polishing your wheels can increase the depth and gloss as well as remove some imperfections

- Protecting your wheels with a sealant is the key to easy maintenance on your wheels

EXTERIOR TRIM

- Having properly cleaned and dressed trim creates more contrast with your paint

- For best results, degrease your trim prior to applying a dressing

- Make sure you are using a dressing that provides UV protection to prevent fading

- Using a brush can help provide a deeper cleaning to your trim pieces

- Old wax build ups can be removed with a degreaser

GLASS

- Use as little glass cleaner as possible to minimize streaking

- Never use ammonia-based glass cleaners on tinted windows

- Use multiple towels to clean your glass, this will help reduce streaking

- Always clean your glass when it is cool to the touch and out of direct sunlight

- Protect your exterior glass to reduce maintenance and to improve visibility during poor weather conditions

- Using a glass polish or distilled white vinegar can help remove water spots on glass

- Before cleaning the glass roll down the window and clean the very top of the glass and the window seal

INTERIOR

- A clean interior shows you take pride in your vehicle

- Cleaning and conditioning your leather on a regular basis will keep the leather looking great year round

- Protect your leather with a product that blocks UV rays

- Leather seats should never feel greasy or oily and avoid any product that adds a shine to the leather

- A scrub brush is arguably the most important tool to clean any fabric

- Microfiber towels are great for interior cleanings because they collect and trap dust particles

- As you exit the vehicle try to not twist on the seat, over time this can remove material from the surface

- Make sure you and your passengers don't have any sharp

- buttons, belts, etc. on your bottom side that can harm the leather

- Keep the interior clean by removing any wrappers, bottles and trash as soon as possible

- Adding an air freshener is an easy way to create a smile

ENGINE

- Many fear cleaning the engine bay when it's actually one of the easiest areas to care for

- It can take as little as 20 minutes to clean and protect the entire engine bay

- The modern day engine bay is so well protected it's quite easy and safe to care for

- A degreaser, protectant and cloths are all you need

- Generally speaking water will not harm the engine bay, it's designed to resist moisture

- Don't use WD-40 or Windex to clean the engine bay

- Clean and protect the engine bay at least twice per year

- Don't forget to care for the hood that gets flipped up

- An EZ Detail Brush can help you reach down in to the engine bay

GENERAL

Always place cord over shoulder when using machine polishers You can use a thin layer of wax around rubber door trim to keep doors from freezing in the winter

Compressed Air, Brush or towel using finger to clean pads while working

ISP alcohol can be used to clean rubber trim & exterior plastics LED Lights will reflex true paint condition as if in sun light

Wax can be applied to windshields & headlights

A very important concept to understand about the pH of a chemical is that it does not change by adding water. For example, a hydrofluoric acid wheel cleaner may have a pH of close to 0. Diluting the acid with water according to the label directions will not change that pH value. What will change is the speed at which the chemical reacts with the surface upon which it is used.

QUIZ'S

CHEMICAL QUIZ

1. The pH scale is based on the higher the number the more acidic it is?
    True or False

2. You can dilute an acid/degreaser with water to change the pH value of chemicals?
    True or False

3. What is the Neutral number on the pH scale?
    a. 0
    b. 7
    c. 14
    d. None of the above

4. Which is appropriate to use on Leather material?
    a. Alkaline cleaner pH 2.5
    b. Alkaline cleaner pH 5.5
    c. Alkaline cleaner pH8.5
    d. Alkaline cleaner pH11.5

5. Which chemical will etch into Wheel paint?
    a. All Purpose Cleaner
    b. Wheel Cleaner (acid)
    c. Mild Degreaser
    d. None of the above

6. Can APC be used to clean leather?
    True or False

7. APC and Degreasers are the same depending on dilution ratio?
    True or False

8. Glass Cleaner would be considered which or the following:
   a. High Acidic
   b. Low Acidic
   c. None of the above

9. Is it safe to mix certain chemicals together to get a stronger cleaning result if mixed with water?
   True or False

10. Spray Wax can be used to do the following:
    a. Clean glass and paint
    b. Used as a decontaminate on paint
    c. Booth D. Neither

GLASS

1. Can you spray the glass and use just one towel?
   True or False

2. The more glass cleaner you use, the better?
   True or False

3. Ammonia based glass cleaners will do which or the following:
   a. Cause streaking
   b. Damage tinted windows
   c. Damage glass treatment
   d. Minimize attracting dirt

4. Which are the best towels to use for cleaning glass:
   a. Micro fiber & Glass Towel
   b. Cotton & Polyester
   c. Cotton & Micro Fiber
   d. None of the above

5.   If diluting concentrated glass cleaner what is the proper dilution ratio:
    a. Adding more water
    b. Using less water
    c. manufacture recommendation
    d. All the above

WASHING QUIZ

1.   How many buckets should you use to wash a vehicles paint; regardless of method or technique your using?
    a. 1
    b. 2
    c. 3
    d. 4

2.   You can use an APC to clay bar a vehicle?
    True or False

3.   You can use glass cleaner to clay bar a vehicle?
    True or False

4.   Can you scratch a vehicle by washing it?
    True or False

5.   Can you scratch a vehicle by drying it?
    True or False

6.   What is the purpose of Grit Guards?
    a. To clean the wash mitt of contaminates
    b. To keep debris and or contaminates from reapplying itself into wash medium
    c. Both
    d. Neither

7. For hard to remove stains on the painted surface of a vehicle; it is recommended to try which of the following first?

    a. Scrub harder using more pressure

    b. Use a clay bay

    c. Use a chemical that is 2.5 on the pH scale

    d. None of the above

8. Can you skip pre-wetting a vehicle before you wash or clay bar it to save time without causing scratches?

    True or False

9. When drying a vehicle after it has been washed; there's still dirt remaining. Can you continue to dry the vehicle and remove the dirt as long as the towel is wet?

    True or False

10. If you drop your clay bar on the ground can is it safe to continue using it?

    True or False

COMPOUND-POLISH-WAX QUIZ

1. Can you use spray wax on interior surfaces of a vehicle?

    True or False

2. Can you use Compound to enhance the gloss & shine on paint surfaces?

    True or False

3. Wax will remove scratches from paint surfaces?

    True or False

4. Paint Sealants will do the following:

    a. Hind light scratches in the paint

    b. Add protection to paint surface

    c. Both

    d. Neither

5. Which of the following can safely be used on interior leather?
   a. Finishing Polish
   b. Light cutting compound
   c. Glass cleaner
   d. None of the above

6. Can you use polish to remove water spots from glass?
   True or false

7. The more Compound – Polish – Wax you use the better?
   True or False

8. The faster your movements when your buffing or polishing; the quicker you'll remove defects and imperfections from paint?
   True or False

9. Which of the following can you use on plastic trim?
   a. Compound
   b. Polish
   c. Wax
   d. None of the above
   e. All the above

10. You can use compound, polish and wax on exhaust tips?
    True or False

WHEELS AND TIRES QUIZ

1. What product is not safe to use on bare metal rims:
   a. Degreaser
   b. All Purpose Cleaner
   c. Low acidic wheel cleaner
   d. High acidic wheel cleaner

2. It is safe to use the same wash medium to wash the vehicle; on the wheels.
   True or False

3. You may use any acidic wheel cleaner without rinsing with water first:

   True or False

4. You can use All Purpose Cleaner as a per-treatment on rims before washing:

   True or False

5. If working in the sun or if the wheels are hot; can you use APC or Degreaser if it is more concentrated:

   True or False

QUIZ ANSWERS

CHEMICALS

1. False
2. False
3. B.
4. D.
5. True
6. False
7. D.
8. False
9. D.
10. D.

COMPOUND-POLISH-WAX

1. True
2. False
3. False
4. C.
5. D.
6. True
7. False
8. False
9. C.
10. True

GLASS

1. False
2. False
3. B.
4. A.
5. C.

WHEELS AND TIRES

1. D.
2. False
3. F.
4. True
5. False

WASHING

1. B.
2. False
3. False
4. True
5. True
6. C.
7. B.
8. False
9. False
10. False

ACKNOWLEDGEMENTS

Buff & Shine Manufacture - Clint Hintz
2139 E Del Amo Blvd, Rancho Dominguez, CA 90220
www.buffandshine.com

Grit Guard - Luan
3690 County Rd 10, Bellefontaine, OH 43311
www.gritguard.com

Solution Finish – Chris West
Hunting Beach, CA.
www.solutionfinish.com

International Detailing Association
2345 Rice St, Ste 220 Saint Paul, MN 55113
www.the-ida.com

Professional Carwashing & Detailing
Rich DiPaolo - Editorial Director

Debra Gorgos - Editor
Auto Detailing News

Bert Youell - Editor
PRO Detailer Magazine

Prentice St. Clair - Detail In Progress
www.detailinprogress.com

Mike Phillips – Director of Training
www.autogeek.net

Josephine Evans
Bettie A. Evans
Angel Michelle Aaron – Service Manager
Jarod Oden – Transportation
Enis White – Transportation

Lorenzo Louden – A Soldier's Redemption
Anthony Falco - Retired
Mike Dickson – PDP
Seth Goss – PDP
Washita Gregory – Entrepreneur

You all have been an inspiration and have aided me somehow in the writing of this book. I am proud and honored to call you family & friends.

Thank you for the support and encouragement you all provided.